BOYNTON BEACH CITY LIBRARY

D1710748

JUN 2 5 2018

LIVING WITH DISEASES AND DISORDERS

Autism and Other Developmental Disorders

LIVING WITH DISEASES AND DISORDERS

ADHD and Other Behavior Disorders

Allergies and Other Immune System Disorders

Asthma, Cystic Fibrosis, and Other Respiratory Disorders

Autism and Other Developmental Disorders

Cancer and Sickle Cell Disease

Cerebral Palsy and Other Traumatic Brain Injuries

Crohn's Disease and Other Digestive Disorders

Depression, Anxiety, and Bipolar Disorders

Diabetes and Other Endocrine Disorders

Migraines and Seizures

Muscular Dystrophy and Other Neuromuscular Disorders

LIVING WITH DISEASES AND DISORDERS

Autism and Other Developmental Disorders

REBECCA SHERMAN

SERIES ADVISOR
HEATHER L. PELLETIER, Ph.D.
Pediatric Psychologist, Hasbro Children's Hospital
Clinical Assistant Professor, Warren Alpert Medical School of Brown University

MASON CREST

Mason Crest
450 Parkway Drive, Suite D
Broomall, PA 19008
www.masoncrest.com

© 2018 by Mason Crest, an imprint of National Highlights, Inc. All rights reserved. No part of this publication may be reproduced or transmitted in any form or by any means, electronic or mechanical, including photocopying, recording, taping, or any information storage and retrieval system, without permission from the publisher.

MTM Publishing, Inc.
435 West 23rd Street, #8C
New York, NY 10011
www.mtmpublishing.com

President: Valerie Tomaselli
Vice President, Book Development: Hilary Poole
Designer: Annemarie Redmond
Copyeditor: Peter Jaskowiak
Editorial Assistant: Leigh Eron

Series ISBN: 978-1-4222-3747-2
Hardback ISBN: 978-1-4222-3751-9
E-Book ISBN: 978-1-4222-8032-4

Library of Congress Cataloging-in-Publication Data
Names: Sherman, Rebecca, author.
Title: Autism and other developmental disorders / by Rebecca Sherman; series consultant,
    Heather Pelletier, PhD, Hasbro Children's Hospital, Alpert Medical School/Brown University.
Description: Broomall, PA : Mason Crest, [2018] | Series: Living with diseases and disorders |
    Audience: Age 12+ | Audience: Grade 7 to 8. | Includes index.
Identifiers: LCCN 2017000434 (print) | LCCN 2017005268 (ebook) | ISBN 9781422237519
    (hardback : alk. paper) | ISBN 9781422280324 (ebook)
Subjects: LCSH: Autism in children—Juvenile literature. | Developmental disabilities—
    Juvenile literature.
Classification: LCC RJ506.A9 S527 2018 (print) | LCC RJ506.A9 (ebook) | DDC 618.92/85882—dc23
LC record available at https://lccn.loc.gov/2017000434

Printed and bound in the United States of America.

First printing
9 8 7 6 5 4 3 2 1

QR CODES AND LINKS TO THIRD PARTY CONTENT
You may gain access to certain third party content ("Third Party Sites") by scanning and using the QR Codes that appear in this publication (the "QR Codes"). We do not operate or control in any respect any information, products or services on such Third Party Sites linked to by us via the QR Codes included in this publication and we assume no responsibility for any materials you may access using the QR Codes. Your use of the QR Codes may be subject to terms, limitations, or restrictions set forth in the applicable terms of use or otherwise established by the owners of the Third Party Sites. Our linking to such Third Party Sites via the QR Codes does not imply an endorsement or sponsorship of such Third Party Sites, or the information, products or services offered on or through the Third Party Sites, nor does it imply an endorsement or sponsorship of this publication by the owners of such Third Party Sites.

TABLE OF CONTENTS

Series Introduction 6

Chapter One: Developmental Disabilities 9

Chapter Two: Autism 25

Chapter Three: Therapies 37

Chapter Four: Finding Strength in Differences 47

Further Reading 57

Series Glossary 58

Index 60

About the Advisor 64

About the Author 64

Photo Credits 64

Key Icons to Look for:

Words to Understand: These words with their easy-to-understand definitions will increase the reader's understanding of the text, while building vocabulary skills.

Sidebars: This boxed material within the main text allows readers to build knowledge, gain insights, explore possibilities, and broaden their perspectives by weaving together additional information to provide realistic and holistic perspectives.

Educational Videos: Readers can view videos by scanning our QR codes, which will provide them with additional educational content to supplement the text. Examples include news coverage, moments in history, speeches, iconic sports moments, and much more.

Text-Dependent Questions: These questions send the reader back to the text for more careful attention to the evidence presented there.

Research Projects: Readers are pointed toward areas of further inquiry connected to each chapter. Suggestions are provided for projects that encourage deeper research and analysis.

Series Glossary of Key Terms: This back-of-the-book glossary contains terminology used throughout the series. Words found here increase the reader's ability to read and comprehend higher-level books and articles in this field.

SERIES INTRODUCTION

According to the Chronic Disease Center at the Centers for Disease Control and Prevention, over 100 million Americans suffer from a chronic illness or medical condition. In other words, they have a health problem that lasts three months or more, affects their ability to perform normal activities, and requires frequent medical care and/or hospitalizations. Epidemiological studies suggest that between 15 and 18 million of those with chronic illness or medical conditions are children and adolescents. That's roughly one out of every four children in the United States.

These young people must exert more time and energy to complete the tasks their peers do with minimal thought. For example, kids with Crohn's disease, ulcerative colitis, or other digestive issues have to plan meals and snacks carefully, to make sure they are not eating food that could irritate their stomachs or cause pain and discomfort. People with cerebral palsy, muscular dystrophy, or other physical limitations associated with a medical condition may need help getting dressed, using the bathroom, or joining an activity in gym class. Those with cystic fibrosis, asthma, or epilepsy may have to avoid certain activities or environments altogether. ADHD and other behavior disorders require the individual to work harder to sustain the level of attention and focus necessary to keep up in school.

Living with a chronic illness or medical condition is not easy. Identifying a diagnosis and adjusting to the initial shock is only the beginning of a long journey. Medications, follow-up appointments and procedures, missed school or work, adjusting to treatment regimens, coping with uncertainty, and readjusting expectations are all hurdles one has to overcome in learning how to live one's best life. Naturally, feelings of sadness or anxiety may set in while learning how to make it all work. This is especially true for young people, who may reach a point in their medical journey when they have to rethink some of their original goals and life plans to better match their health reality.

Chances are, you know people who live this reality on a regular basis. It is important to remember that those affected by chronic illness are family members, neighbors, friends, or maybe even our own doctors. They are likely navigating the demands of the day a little differently, as they balance the specific accommodations necessary to manage their illness. But they have the same desire to be productive and included as those who are fortunate not to have a chronic illness.

This set provides valuable information about the most common childhood chronic illnesses, in language that is engaging and easy for students to grasp. Each chapter highlights important vocabulary words and offers text-dependent questions to help assess comprehension. Meanwhile, educational videos (available by scanning QR codes) and research projects help connect the text to the outside world.

Our mission with this set is twofold. First, the volumes provide a go-to source for information about chronic illness for young people who are living with particular conditions. Each volume in this set strives to provide reliable medical information and practical advice for living day-to-day with various challenges. Second, we hope these volumes will also help kids without chronic illness better understand and appreciate how people with health challenges live. After all, if one in four young people is managing a health condition, it's safe to assume that the majority of our youth already know someone with a chronic illness, whether they realize it or not.

With the growing presence of social media, bullying is easier than ever before. It's vital that young people take a moment to stop and think about how they are more similar to kids with health challenges than they are different. Poor understanding and low tolerance for individual differences are often the platforms for bullying and noninclusive behavior, both in person and online. Living with Diseases and Disorders strives to close the gap of misunderstanding.

The ultimate solution to the bullying problem is surely an increase in empathy. We hope these books will help readers better understand and appreciate not only the daily struggles of people living with chronic conditions, but their triumphs as well.

—Heather Pelletier, Ph.D.
Hasbro Children's Hospital
Warren Alpert Medical School of Brown University

WORDS TO UNDERSTAND

atypical: different from the usual.

chromosome: a double helix made of DNA; it contains genes.

compelled: forced or pressured to do something.

continuum: a collection of values or qualities that change a little bit from one to the next, but a lot from one end to the other.

disability: a condition that restricts a person's ability to do essential activities.

impair: damage, injure, or make worse.

prevalence: how common or uncommon a condition is in a population.

spectrum: a way of classifying information or things along a continuum.

tic: an involuntary repeated behavior or movement of muscles.

CHAPTER ONE

Developmental Disabilities

Imagine living in a world where noises are too loud, lights shine too brightly, and people behave in ways you can't understand, no matter how hard you try. You might feel like you're in a foreign country. Bombarded by customs and conversations that don't make any sense, you might feel overwhelmed, exhausted, or anxious a lot of the time. You would probably feel different from everyone around you. You might prefer being alone in your room to going out. Alone, you wouldn't feel different or confused. For someone with a developmental disability, this is not an imaginary scenario.

Autism is probably the best-known developmental disability—you may know someone who lives with it, or you might have it yourself. Other developmental disabilities include dyslexia and Down syndrome. We'll talk more about these and other conditions later in this chapter.

Understanding Developmental Disabilities

Developmental disabilities can **impair** or affect how a person moves, thinks, speaks, learns, or behaves. They are usually diagnosed in infancy or early childhood, when the human brain is developing rapidly. There is generally no cure for a developmental disability—it lasts for a person's entire life. But the effects of a developmental disability vary hugely from one disability to another, and from one person to another. Some people with a developmental disability may struggle to learn how to manage basic daily activities, like

Different types of therapy are available for people with different developmental challenges.

WHAT'S IN A NAME?

The word *autism* has only existed since 1911, when the Swiss psychiatrist Eugen Bleuler coined it, using the Greek word *autos*, or "self." He used the word to describe certain patients with an advanced form of schizophrenia, a brain disorder that causes people to suffer from intense and vivid delusions. Completely absorbed in their delusions, Bleuler's patients paid no attention to the real world.

In 1943 the psychiatrist Leo Kanner borrowed Bleuler's term to describe the behavior of young patients who were self-contained in a very different way. These children were unable to form emotional or social connections with other people. Instead, they engaged in repetitive behaviors, saying or doing the same things over and over again. In their lack of interest and attention to others, these children seemed to Kanner to be trapped in their own selves, as though stuck inside a shell. He called this condition "extreme autistic aloneness."

Because both men used the same term to describe what they saw in their patients, doctors and psychologists assumed they were describing the same disorder. A book called the *Diagnostic and Statistical Manual of Mental Disorders* (known as the *DSM*) classified many autistic behaviors as "childhood schizophrenia." Not until 1980 was "infantile autism" listed as its own disorder. That name was changed again in 1994, to "pervasive developmental disorders." The most recent revision of the *DSM* (the *DSM-5*), published in 2013, switched to the name "autistic spectrum disorder."

dressing, eating, or otherwise taking care of themselves. Other people with developmental disabilities may have no trouble with daily life, but have difficulty in one particular area at school. That difficulty doesn't stop them from succeeding or even excelling in other ways. No matter how severe or mild a kid's developmental disabilities are, specialized therapies and training can help.

There are three main categories of developmental disabilities:

- intellectual disabilities
- learning disabilities
- autism spectrum disorder (ASD).

A person with an intellectual disability has trouble learning, remembering, and understanding. He or she may struggle to master simple tasks, and score below average on tests meant to measure intelligence. At school, someone with an intellectual disability may spend most of the day in special education classes with a dedicated aide.

Someone who has a learning disability struggles with one or more learning skills that are necessary to succeed at school. Kids with learning disabilities are just as intelligent as anyone else. They just may need extra time and tutoring to do the same schoolwork.

ASD is arguably the most complex developmental disability, and it can look very different from individual to individual. An autistic person may be severely disabled and need to be in special education classes with a full-time aide. Another autistic person may have social challenges to overcome but excel in advanced classes. How well those with autism function depends on both the number of disabilities they have and the severity of each disability.

It can be tough to generalize about such a diverse group of people with so many different levels of ability. But one thing holds true across the board. People with developmental disabilities often need support, aid, and understanding in order to live their lives to the fullest—just like people without developmental disabilities. Whether or not you have a developmental

Having a learning disability does not mean someone is less intelligent—it just means that studying may be more challenging for that person than it is for others.

disability, support from your family, friends, school, and community will help you achieve your goals.

Developmental Disorders at a Glance

An estimated one out of every six children in the United States has at least one developmental disability. The most common type is learning disabilities.

Children with dysgraphia have trouble with writing.

The government agency responsible for keeping track of the prevalence of diseases and disorders in the United States, the Centers for Disease Control and Prevention (CDC), estimates that 7.66 percent of children have a specific learning disability. A specific learning disability indicates that a person's brain processes or interprets a particular kind of information

EDUCATIONAL VIDEO

Scan this code for a video about autism and communication.

differently than most people. Here are some of the most common learning disabilities:

- **Dyslexia** causes difficulties in learning to read, write, and spell.
- **Dysgraphia** makes it difficult to write by hand.
- **Dyscalculia** affects the ability to understand numbers and tell time.
- **Auditory processing disorder** impairs a person's ability to make sense of sound. A subtype, language processing disorder, causes problems understanding spoken language.
- **Visual perception/visual motor deficit** affects the ability to understand things a person sees, and the ability to draw.
- **Nonverbal learning disabilities** are diagnosed when someone has excellent verbal skills but poor physical coordination, an inability to read social situations, or trouble understanding what they see.

Intellectual disabilities used to be called "mental retardation," but these days that term is considered offensive and is not used anymore. Listed here are some types of intellectual disability:

- **Down syndrome** is caused by a genetic condition; it occurs when the fertilized egg contains an extra chromosome. The presence of

In the United States, about 6,000 babies are born with Down syndrome every year.

the extra chromosome causes the fetus to develop in atypical ways, affecting the brain and other parts of the body.

- **Fragile X syndrome** occurs when the developing fetus has a mutation of a particular gene on the X chromosome. Boys are twice as likely as girls to have fragile X syndrome. Boys are also more likely to have more severe disability due to fragile X syndrome. Kids with fragile X syndrome are more likely to have autism, too.

- **Fetal alcohol spectrum disorder** affects the development of the brain when a fetus is exposed to alcohol. It is the reason why women are advised not to drink beer, wine, or liquor while pregnant.

- Exposure to certain toxins or diseases as a fetus, infant, or very young child may cause **intellectual disability**.
- **Brain injuries** suffered at birth or in childhood can result in intellectual disability.

HOMES FOR THE FEEBLE-MINDED

In the 19th and 20th centuries, families of children with developmental disabilities were encouraged to send those children away to institutions that advertised themselves as "homes for the feeble-minded." Many doctors believed that children with developmental disabilities suffered from "idiocy" or "insanity" and should not be allowed to live in their own homes. They argued that children with disabilities would grow up to be permanent burdens on their families and society.

Persuaded by these arguments, many families did as they were advised. But the children who were sent away to institutions often never returned. Conditions inside these institutions were sometimes like strict schools or hospitals, but just as often they were more like work camps or even prisons. Some children were underfed, overworked, abused, and subjected to dubious medical treatments that we'd now consider torture. While some institutions did their best to be caring homes for developmentally disabled people, others were true houses of horrors where untold numbers of people suffered and died. Most of these institutions were shut down decades ago, and many of them are now ruins. But their shameful history should not be forgotten.

The final category of developmental disabilities, autism spectrum disorder (ASD), is also known as autism spectrum conditions or simply as autism. Within the category of ASD are people with a very wide range of abilities. That's why autism is described as a **spectrum**.

Understanding the Spectrum

You're probably familiar with the spectrum of colors in a rainbow. The colors of light in a prism don't have a sharp line separating one from the next. Red blends into orange, which blends into yellow—but red looks very different from yellow. The colors form a **continuum** in which it can be hard to distinguish the difference between two points right next to one another, though it's easy to tell the difference between two points that are far apart.

The two ends of the autism spectrum look so different from one another that, not so long ago, they were considered to be different disorders. The profoundly disabled end was called Kanner's syndrome, after Leo Kanner, the psychiatrist who identified it in children brought to his Baltimore clinic in the 1940s. These children had intellectual disabilities and were generally unable to care for themselves. The other end of the spectrum was called Asperger's syndrome, after Hans Asperger, the Austrian pediatrician who first described it in 1944 as an affliction that made children seem like "little professors." People on this end of the spectrum may display unusual intelligence, even genius-level intelligence, particularly in the fields of science, technology, math, and engineering. But it's important to remember that neither end of the spectrum defines autism. People with ASD can and do fall in between the extremes, being neither geniuses nor intellectually disabled. What distinguishes people with autism isn't whether they seem "smart" or not, but how their brains work to process information. Brain scans show that people with autism process information differently than people without autism. That affects how someone with autism thinks, behaves, and feels.

To understand the idea of a spectrum, think of a rainbow in which colors are closely related and blend one into the next, but each one is also unique.

Developmental Disabilities and Other Disorders

There are several conditions that are often found in people who have autism and certain other developmental disabilities. Epilepsy is a brain disorder that causes seizures. Depending on the severity of the seizures and the situation in which they occur, the seizures can result in brain damage or other serious

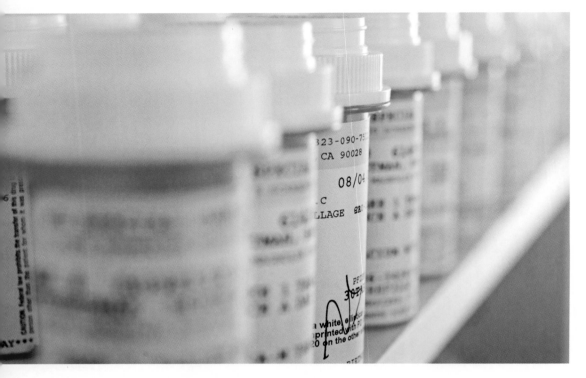

There are many types of anti-seizure medications. They can be life-saving for people with epilepsy.

injury. Epilepsy does not have a single cause—many different diseases and disorders can cause epileptic seizures. Epilepsy is much more common in people with ASD than it is in the general population. In some cases, epilepsy may develop before symptoms of autism are apparent. Epilepsy is also more common in people with Down syndrome and fragile X syndrome. People who have epilepsy along with a developmental disability are more likely to have severe intellectual disabilities.

People with autism are also more likely to suffer from a genetic condition called tuberous sclerosis complex (TSC). TSC causes multiple tumors to grow in the brain, heart, lungs, kidneys, skin, and other organs. The tumors are not cancerous and do not spread. But they may interfere with normal brain functioning. Headaches, blurred vision, seizures, epilepsy, and developmental delays and disabilities affect people with TSC.

Tourette syndrome (or Tourette's) is a developmental disability that causes people to feel compelled to make the same movements or sounds over and over again. These repetitive behaviors are called tics. Common simple tics include sniffling and throat-clearing, blinking, shrugging, grimacing, and jerking of the head or shoulders. More complex tics involve a series of motions, or spoken words or phrases.

You may have seen a character in a TV show or movie who supposedly has Tourette's. In fiction, Tourette syndrome usually causes characters to swear a lot or say other socially inappropriate things. But in reality, only about 15 percent of people with Tourette syndrome actually have that symptom. Mild cases of Tourette syndrome may even not require treatment, but more severe cases may be treated with medication or behavioral therapy.

Tourette syndrome is not very common, but it is more common in people with other developmental disabilities. Most kids with Tourette's have at least one other developmental disability. Nearly 50 percent of people with Tourette's have a learning disability, and 35 percent of people who have Tourette syndrome also have

A portrait of George Gilles de la Tourette. He wrote about a condition that he called a "maladie de tics" that later became known as Tourette syndrome.

DOWN SYNDROME

Down syndrome is one of the most common causes of intellectual disability, affecting 1 in every 800 babies. Unlike many other developmental disabilities, it has a very specific single cause. Human beings have 23 pairs of chromosomes, which contain our genes. Each pair contains one chromosome from a person's mother and one from a person's father. But in Down syndrome, one set of chromosomes is a trio instead of a pair. People with Down syndrome have three copies of the 21st chromosome.

This extra chromosome has several effects on a person's development. People with Down syndrome often have distinctive physical characteristics, like slightly flattened faces, skin folds around the eyes, small mouths and hands, and low muscle tone. They may speak poorly, and often have vision and hearing problems. They may have a serious heart defect, which may require surgery to repair. They grow and develop more slowly. While intellectual disability is common, it can vary from person to person. Some people with Down syndrome are severely impaired. Others have only mild intellectual disabilities. Up to 10 percent of people with Down syndrome also have ASD. As adults, some people with Down syndrome need full-time aid and support. Others work and live independently for the most part.

autism spectrum disorder. Attention-deficit hyperactivity disorder, obsessive-compulsive disorder, speech disorders, and anxiety are also common in people with Tourette's. Diseases and disorders that are often present together are called *co-occurring conditions*.

Text-Dependent Questions

1. How can developmental disabilities affect a person?
2. What are three categories of developmental disabilities?
3. Why is the word "spectrum" used to describe autism spectrum disorder?

Research Project

Kids with intellectual disabilities live in every community. Ask your teachers or school administrators if there are kids with intellectual disabilities at your school. If you can, talk to one of these kids, or to their special education teachers. Find out what their school day is like. How is it like yours? How is it different?

WORDS TO UNDERSTAND

articulate: being able to speak one's thoughts clearly and well.

assistive device: a tool that helps someone with a disability perform a particular task, like speaking, walking, seeing, or hearing.

environmental factors: anything that affects how people live, develop, or grow. Climate, diet, and pollution are examples.

figurative language: language that uses one thing to say or signify something else, like metaphors and similes.

genetic mutations: changes in the composition or order of genes on a chromosome.

hormones: substances produced by the body to send messages and instructions to organs and tissues.

neurotypical: having a brain that processes information the same way that most people do.

psychiatric: related to mental illness.

stimming: an informal term for voluntary repeated movements associated with autism.

CHAPTER TWO

Autism

Autism was once thought of as a rare disorder. But the number of people diagnosed with autism has risen steeply over the past 40 years. In 2002, the CDC estimated that 1 in every 150 children had some form of autism. Ten years later, the estimate had risen to 1 in every 68 children. A national survey conducted in 2014 found that 1 in every 45 children in the United States had some form of autism.

It's not clear why autism rates have risen so sharply. Scientists think part of the reason may be that media attention and advocacy campaigns have made doctors, families, and schools much more aware of ASD. Children are much more likely to be screened for it than they used to be. One thing is clear: people with autism exist in every community. Autism affects rich kids, poor kids, and kids in between, as well as people from every ethnic group. Worldwide, between 1 and 2 percent of the population has some form of autism.

Causes of ASD

Scientists believe that ASD is caused by **genetic mutations** combined with **environmental factors**. There is no single gene for autism, and no single cause. Researchers have identified many different genetic mutations that appear to be associated with ASD. That means these mutations are often found in people with ASD. But no one knows if they cause ASD, or how they might do so. A person with ASD can have more than one of these mutations. The more genetic mutations a person has, the more likely that person is to be severely impaired.

Some of these genetic mutations are inherited, which is why ASD tends to run in families. But some genetic mutations occur randomly. They are called *de novo* or acquired mutations, as opposed to inherited mutations. Parents who are over 40

ASD expresses itself differently in different people—there is no way to tell if someone has ASD just by looking at them.

UNDERSTANDING PREVALENCE

Although the media sometimes refers to autism as an "epidemic," the truth is we actually don't know whether more people have it now than in the past. Why not? The answer has a lot to do with how much our understanding of autism has changed over the past 70 years.

Imagine you've been asked to survey a flower garden and count the roses in bloom. There's one problem: you're not really sure what roses look like. You ask a gardener, who says, "Roses are red flowers." So you count all the red flowers in the garden.

The next day, another gardener tells you that roses are pink flowers. Whoops! You go back to the garden and count all the pink flowers.

A week later, a third gardener explains that roses can be red *or* pink. You make a fresh count of all the red and pink flowers in the garden.

A month later, a master gardener sends you a book of photos of flowers. Now you see that roses can be almost any color. But you're embarrassed to discover that not all red or pink flowers are roses. Some are poppies, or carnations. You go back to the garden, carefully examine all the flowers, and count the roses.

If somebody asked you how many roses are in the garden, you'd now have four very different answers, because each time you counted something different. Because of the way the definition of autism has changed over time, estimates of how many people have had autism in the past compared to today have the same problem as your flower garden survey.

years old when they have kids are more likely to pass on *de novo* genetic mutations. This means kids born to older parents are at higher risk to have autism.

Boys are two to three times more likely to be autistic than girls. This leads some scientists to believe that autism may be linked to exposure to certain **hormones** that are more present in boys than in girls. But no one has yet proved for sure whether hormones affect autism. Scientists caution that autism may just look a little different in girls than in boys. In other words, it's possible that girls are less likely to be *diagnosed* with ASD, but not less likely to have it. Scientists are still trying to determine if other environmental factors affect the development of autism. They are looking at air pollution, pesticides, hormone-like chemicals in the environment, and other factors. It may be many years before they find a definitive answer.

Autism Defined

Doctors can confirm you have the flu by running a lab test to check for the presence of the flu virus. But there is no simple yes-or-no test a doctor can give for autism. Instead, doctors and psychologists evaluate a person's behavior and patterns of thought. The tools they use include direct observation, interviews with parents or caregivers, reports on the person's behavior from teachers and school administrators, and a medical examination. All of these bits of information fit together like puzzle pieces, revealing an overall picture.

By definition, people with autism differ from other people in two major ways. First, they have trouble communicating with others, particularly in face-to-face situations. They may have trouble expressing themselves verbally. Some people with autism cannot use spoken language at all. They may be able to understand what is said around them. They may be able to communicate using an **assistive device**. They may use a stand-alone or tablet-based app that allows them to communicate simple concepts with icons and pictures. Or they may use a computerized voice to speak for them.

There is no quick test for ASD; patients need to be evaluated by doctors who are trained to spot the signals.

Other kids who struggle with spoken language may be able to write eloquently about complex issues using a keyboard and computer. But they might not understand when other people talk about emotions and feelings. They may struggle to identify or express their own emotions in words. Being unable to communicate feelings in words can be extremely frustrating. Some kids may act up, throw tantrums, and even hurt themselves or their caregivers because they get so frustrated when they can't make their needs understood.

Not everyone with autism has trouble speaking, though. People on the high-functioning end of the spectrum may be **articulate** when talking about subjects that interest them. Often, the subject of their interest involves a lot of detailed information that can be sorted into intricate categories, like baseball scores or Pokémon characters. They may talk about their interests at great length, and they may not notice if the person they're talking to seems bored or tries to change the subject. This is one reason why even high-functioning people with autism may seem odd or awkward at times.

Sometimes people with ASD have difficulty "reading" the meaning of facial expressions.

People with autism may also have trouble understanding **figurative language**. They may misunderstand if you use exaggeration for effect ("This is the worst day ever!"), metaphors and similes ("This day is like a disaster zone"), and sarcasm ("Well, *this* was a great day"). They may really enjoy puns, but fail to get jokes that rely on irony, emotion, or context.

EDUCATIONAL VIDEO

Scan this code for a video about autism.

Most people with autism find it difficult to understand nonverbal communication, like body language and facial expressions. **Neurotypical** is a word used to describe people who don't have autism. If you're neurotypical, you notice a lot about the emotions of the people around you. It's obvious to you when someone is angry, or upset, or bored. You interpret facial expressions and body language—often without even thinking about it. You respond differently to a friend who looks mad than to one who seems happy. But if you are autistic, you may not be able to read facial expressions or body language. Some people with autism describe themselves as "face-blind," meaning that they can see faces but they can't "see" what the expressions mean. The inability to read other people's faces and emotions can leave autistic people bewildered in social situations. They may say or do things that are inappropriate to the situation.

These problems with social communication may be present from birth. Sometimes the problems take time to appear, not showing up until a child's second birthday. Neurotypical babies often look directly at their parents' faces, cooing or babbling in response to a parent talking. But babies with ASD might avoid looking at faces. They may not coo or babble. Toddlers with ASD may use fewer words than other children at the same age, or they may not speak at all.

THE ANTI-VACCINE SCAM

In 1998, an English physician named Andrew Wakefield and several colleagues published a study of 12 children who had been diagnosed with autism. Eight of the children showed symptoms soon after receiving a vaccination for three childhood diseases: measles, mumps, and rubella. The study itself did not prove that the vaccination, known as the MMR vaccine, had anything to do with autism. But Wakefield gave press conferences and made a promotional video asserting that the MMR vaccine might actually cause autism. This assertion received wide coverage in the news. Frightened parents in England and in the United States refused to vaccinate their children. As a result, outbreaks of all three diseases sickened children in both countries.

Other scientists rushed to research this supposed link between vaccines and autism. It became one of the most thoroughly researched questions in modern medicine. But study after study turned up no evidence that vaccines had anything to do with autism. Eventually, it came out that Wakefield had lied about some of the data in his original study. It also turned out that Wakefield had taken money from lawyers who planned to sue vaccine manufacturers and needed help in their case. Wakefield lost his medical license and was no longer allowed to work as a doctor in England.

A neurotypical toddler might be eager to share things, bringing a new toy over to a parent or pointing at a dog on the street so that a parent looks at the dog, too. Toddlers with ASD don't tend to share what they are interested in or what they are doing. They may seem happiest to be left alone. Unlike typically developing children, they show little interest in let's-pretend games or role-playing. They may spend a great deal of time organizing toys by size or color.

Routine and Repetition

The second defining characteristic of autistic spectrum disorder is an unusual need to repeat things or experiences. To a degree, this is common among all young children. Little kids often get very attached to routines. They might only eat certain foods, or wear a favorite hat everywhere, or demand the same three bedtime stories in the same order every single night.

But for kids with ASD, these patterns of repetition can be extreme. The need for routine may persist as the child gets older, and even into adulthood. For more severely impaired children, a need for sameness and predictability can mean they get very upset by little changes in their environment. They may have

Some people with ASD like to organize things by size or color.

AUTISM SPECTRUM QUOTIENT

Do you enjoy social situations? Do you find it easy to make up stories? Do you notice details that other people miss? Is it hard for you if there's a sudden change in your plans? Do you easily remember other people's birthdays?

These are the kind of questions some specialists use to assess whether a person should be evaluated for autism spectrum disorder. For each question, one answer is more common among people with autism. (For the questions above, the answers that someone with ASD might give are: no, no, yes, yes, yes.)

It's normal for a person without autism to share some of the preferences and personality traits that are considered autistic. That's because each of these traits exists as a range—or a spectrum—in the general population. There is no right or wrong answer to any of the questions. There is also no single answer that "makes" a person autistic. Rather, diagnostic questionnaires like the Autistic Spectrum Quotient give one point for every answer common to ASD. A score above a certain threshold does not mean that a person has ASD. But it does increase the likelihood that further evaluation will result in a diagnosis of ASD.

tantrums for what seems like no reason, simply because of some tiny change in routine that others might not even notice.

They may also be distressed by certain noises, textures, or sights. Many people with autism process sensory information differently. They can be very upset by sounds that don't bother most neurotypical people. They might have strong reactions to certain sights or lights. They might feel that a pair of jeans is unbearably scratchy against their skin, and only wear sweatpants. On the other hand, some people with ASD need more sensory stimulation than usual. They may be drawn to loud, piercing noises, or seek out rough surfaces to touch.

People with autism may find the repetition of certain physical movements very soothing or enjoyable. For example, they may wave their hands in certain fixed ways over and over again, or rock back and forth. This practice is called self-stimulation, or **stimming** for short. There is nothing harmful about stimming, but people with autism are sometimes told to avoid stimming in public so as not to draw attention to themselves.

People with autism are at greater risk for repetitive self-harming behaviors, like banging one's head against a wall. In severe cases, medications that treat **psychiatric** disorders like anxiety or obsessive-compulsive disorder may be used to control self-harming impulses.

Text-Dependent Questions

1. What do we know about the prevalence of autistic spectrum disorder?
2. Name two ways someone with autism might struggle in a social situation.
3. How might a toddler with autism differ from a typical toddler?

Research Project

Look over this guide from the Autism Society about teens with autism: www.autism-society.org/wp-content/uploads/2014/04/NEWasa-growing_up-teen-final-rev.pdf. After reading about how teens with ASD are unique, how would you go about being a good friend to someone with ASD? List three things you would do, and three things you'd avoid.

WORDS TO UNDERSTAND

accommodations: arrangements or adjustments to help a person manage a disability at school.

behavior training: a type of therapy that uses positive reinforcement to teach what to do in different situations.

deviation: different from what is expected.

echolalia: a condition in which one repeats overheard words or phrases.

inconclusive: still in doubt, unproven.

nutritional supplements: pills, powders, or liquids meant to supply some vitamin or other nutrient that's either missing or inadequately present in the diet.

occupational therapy: a type of therapy that teaches one how to accomplish tasks and activities in daily life.

speech-language pathologist: someone who treats disorders involving communication, language, speaking, and swallowing.

CHAPTER THREE

Therapies

Crowds in the hallway between classes. A noisy lunchroom. A classroom assignment in which groups of kids have to talk to one another about the reading. Some kids with ASD can navigate challenges like these, though it might take a lot of effort. Others kids with ASD struggle with these situations. It depends on their degree of impairment. One person on the high-functioning end of the spectrum may manage well enough to succeed in a regular school environment. But someone on the low-functioning end of the spectrum may get frightened, anxious, or aggressive at any **deviation** from his or her preferred environment, even at home.

But treatment can often help people with ASD learn better coping skills, no matter which end of the spectrum they are on. And that can allow them to participate more fully at home, at school, and in the community.

Medication and Nutrition

Unlike many other disorders, autism is not generally treated with medication, though someone with autism may take medication to treat other conditions.

Research is being done to discover whether some medications may ease some of the symptoms associated with ASD.

Other researchers are investigating whether or not some kind of special diet or **nutritional supplements** might improve the quality of life for people with ASD. Right now, the science about medications and diet is **inconclusive**. Medications do seem to help with some conditions often associated with autism, like anxiety and attention-deficit hyperactivity disorder (ADHD). Diets and supplements may ease digestive problems reported by many kids with autism. But medication, diets, and supplements do not appear to affect the core impairments of autism.

Some symptoms of ASD can be identified as early as age two.

Therapy to Change Behavior

Most doctors and psychologists recommend a program of treatment involving **behavior training** and therapy.

Some evidence suggests that treatment is more effective when begun early, so children as young as two or three may begin therapy as soon as possible after being diagnosed with ASD. There are many different types of therapy that can help children with ASD, depending on their age and degree of impairment. In general, therapies help develop the ability to interact with other people and respond more flexibly to the challenges of daily life.

Speech-Language Therapy

To learn social communication skills, young children diagnosed with autism often begin one-on-one therapy to develop their ability to pay attention to, imitate, and engage with other people. A specialist called a **speech-language pathologist** teaches both verbal and nonverbal communication skills. Some children may have developmental delays that make it hard for them to physically control their mouths and tongues. Speech therapy can help these children acquire the physical skills required to speak clearly. But because children with autism may not be naturally comfortable with language, they may need training to use language to express and communicate their thoughts, even if they are physically capable of speech. Kids with ASD who can't speak at all may learn how to communicate using pictures or assistive devices.

A speech-language pathologist can also help kids with ASD learn how to handle social settings and conversation. People with ASD tend to be good at focusing on details, so kids with ASD are often given very detailed, step-by-step instructions on how to respond to a given situation. A therapist may spend many hours a week coaching an autistic child to say hello when a new person enters

Therapists design programs to help patients with ASD work on specific skills.

the room. It might take many more hours to teach the child to respond properly when asked, "What is your name?"

Focusing on details can make it hard for some people with autism to recognize how two things that are a little bit different can also be alike. A typical person doesn't have to be told that the question "What is your name?" is similar to the question "What are you called?" But a kid with autism might have to practice responding to both questions before understanding that the same answer works for both.

BULLYING AND DISABILITY

Kids with developmental disabilities often have to deal with feeling they are different from other kids. That difference can take many forms. Someone with autism may feel different because he doesn't understand how other kids make friends. Someone with a learning disability like dyslexia or dyscalculia may feel different because she has trouble doing schoolwork at the same time or in the same way as the other students in her class. Someone with Down syndrome may feel different because he doesn't understand things as quickly or completely as other kids.

It makes life even harder for people with disabilities if they are singled out or bullied for being different. Kids with developmental disabilities have the same feelings as everyone else. They want to feel liked. They like to feel useful. They enjoy feeling like they belong. They appreciate kindness and friendship. Standing up to bullies is one of the most important things you can do to make your home, school, and community more welcoming to kids with developmental disabilities, and to their families, too. By being respectful and considerate of differences, you can help create places where everyone can thrive.

Some people with ASD have a condition called echolalia, in which they repeat memorized phrases or sentences that they've heard other people say. These phrases may be used over and over, out of context, or in inappropriate situations. But they can also be useful for someone who has a very hard time figuring out how to use words in context. Having a collection of memorized phrases or sentences can make it easier for a person with ASD to think of what to say. Speech therapy can help a person with ASD be a better judge of how and when to use a phrase or sentence they've memorized.

Other Types of Therapy

Some people with autism and other developmental disabilities, like Down syndrome, have poor muscle tone, physical coordination, or motor skills. Physical or **occupational therapy** can help a child learn how to tackle skills requiring physical coordination. Physical therapy might help very young children learn how to sit up, roll over, walk, and run. Older children might learn how to skip, jump, swim, or play with a ball. Occupational therapy might help someone learn how to put on a shirt, pants, or shoes. It might teach someone how to draw and write using a pencil or crayon. Using a knife and fork, cutting with scissors, and brushing teeth are other physical skills that someone might need help mastering.

Developmental Disabilities at School

The Individuals with Disabilities Education Act (IDEA), a law first passed in 1975, states that all students with disabilities are entitled to a free, appropriate public education that meets their unique needs. By the terms of this law, public schools are legally required to provide special education **accommodations** to students with developmental disabilities.

Students may receive extra help as part of special education classes, by a trained aide in a regular classroom, or as enrichment programs after or away from school. Students with developmental disabilities should have an Individualized Education Program (IEP) that specifies what special education

Researchers have estimated that the treatment and education of kids with ASD can cost about $17,000 more than neurotypical kids.

services and accommodations they receive. These will vary, depending on the person and the disability. Someone with dyslexia might receive services in the form of time spent working one-on-one with a therapist who teaches reading skills using special techniques. Accommodations for that person might include using audiobooks and earphones when other kids in the class are reading, answering test questions verbally instead of having to write them down, or getting extra time to read and write assignments or tests.

THE INDIVIDUALS WITH DISABILITIES EDUCATION ACT

For most of American history, children with developmental disabilities had no guaranteed access to educational services. Kids with severe developmental disabilities often had no education at all. Sent away to institutions or hidden away at home, they never attended school. Parents were told it was a waste of time to try teaching severely impaired children—they were, authorities said, incapable of learning. Kids with more mild disabilities might attend school, but if they struggled with the work, teachers might label them "lazy" or "stupid." Ashamed and defeated, kids often believed their teachers' verdict. Many dropped out without finishing high school.

That began to change for the better in the 1950s, when parents of children with developmental disabilities fought for access to educational services. They pushed for new laws providing federal funding and support for teacher training and programs for kids with disabilities. In 1972, Congress passed Public Law 94-142, the Education for All Handicapped Children Act, which guaranteed a free, appropriate public education to disabled children. The name of the law was changed in 1997 to the Individuals with Disabilities Education Act (IDEA). Thanks to IDEA, school districts are required to provide effective educational services to kids with developmental disabilities from preschool through high school.

Kids with intellectual disabilities, like Down syndrome and fragile X syndrome, are also entitled to a free and appropriate public education under the law. IDEA further specifies that kids with disabilities should be educated in the "least restrictive environment." That means that they should be included in classrooms and educational opportunities with nondisabled students whenever possible. A kid with an intellectual disability may be in a regular classroom (often assisted by an aide) for homeroom, gym, and art, but attend a special education class for the rest of the day.

EDUCATIONAL VIDEO

Scan this code for a video about dyslexia.

Text-Dependent Questions

1. What sort of situations might be hard for a person with autism? Why?
2. What do doctors recommend to treat the impairments of autism?
3. What are some of the things a speech-language pathologist might help a person do?

Research Project

Learn more about dyslexia from http://kidshealth.org/en/kids/dyslexia.html. Think about what you do in school every day. How would you change your classroom lessons to make them easier for a kid with dyslexia to learn?

WORDS TO UNDERSTAND

advocacy: work to support a cause or a change in public policy.

enhanced: increased or improved.

neurodiversity: the idea that there is wide natural variation in the way human brains develop, such that different learning and processing styles should all be considered normal.

CHAPTER FOUR

Finding Strength in Differences

Developmental disabilities can hinder a person's ability to do a lot of things. But that's not the whole story. Sometimes, different ways of thinking and processing information can be an advantage. Some people with ASD or learning disabilities have an **enhanced** ability to approach problems from new and illuminating perspectives that wouldn't occur to a more typical person.

Researchers think that a number of major scientific and technical discoveries may have been made by autistic people with the ability to think differently. Much has been written analyzing the behavior of long-dead famous scientists and innovators for signs of autism. While there's no way to know for sure whether any particular historical figure had ASD, we do know that there has been a real change in how people think about developmental disabilities in general, and ASD in particular. Where autistic people might have once been locked away in an institution, they are now recognized for having valuable contributions to make to schools, communities, and even corporations.

Personality aspects of ASD can sometimes make some people better at certain jobs than neurotypical people.

Autistic People Help Make New Technology

Some personality traits of autistic people may be an advantage in certain jobs, especially ones that involve a lot of repetition and attention to detail. Jobs like computer programmer, lab scientist, and safety engineer require those qualities, as do many others, particularly in science, technology, engineering, and math (STEM). Companies like Microsoft and the German software corporation SAP have begun actively recruiting people with autism to fill certain positions. Managers acknowledge that people with autism may need support in handling communication and interaction with their coworkers. But their many strengths more than make up for any special accommodations they might need.

One popular theory about the apparent rise in the prevalence of autism suggests that people on the high-functioning end of the autism spectrum get jobs in STEM fields, then end up marrying one another and passing down a genetic predisposition to autism. Careful research does not seem to confirm this theory—rates of autism are not higher in communities where a lot of people work in science and technology. But it is certainly true that people with autism have helped drive innovation in science and technology.

According to the journalist Steve Silberman, the first electronic bulletin board was developed in Berkeley, California, by a man with ASD named Lee Felsenstein. His creation allowed people to use a computer to connect with other people who shared their interests. It was perhaps the earliest example of online social networking.

New Technologies Help Autistic People

Computers and online social networking have allowed people with developmental disabilities to learn and connect in new and effective ways. Someone with ASD can use social media to communicate with other people around the world without having to read body language or use spoken language. Even emojis can be very helpful for

TEMPLE GRANDIN

Dr. Temple Grandin is a professor of animal sciences at Colorado State University. She also has autism. Born in 1947, she came of age in an era when parents were still being advised to put children with developmental disabilities in an institution. But Grandin's wealthy mother disregarded that advice. Instead, she got three-year-old Temple speech therapy and paid for special educational services at expensive private schools.

Though Grandin was bullied in school, she eventually found a supportive science teacher. One summer, helping out on her aunt's Arizona ranch, she noticed that agitated calves calmed down when held in a "squeeze" chute—a device that keeps calves still when they are getting vaccinated. She wondered if something similar might help her calm down when her autistic hypersensitivity made her overwhelmed and upset. Her science teacher helped her construct a squeeze machine for herself, and it worked!

Inspired by that experience, she went on to a very successful career, designing humane equipment and buildings for cattle and other livestock. An essay by the best-selling author Oliver Sacks about how she turned her autistic insights into a career made her a household name. Since then she has written multiple books, given many interviews, been named by *Time* magazine as one of the 100 most influential people in the world, and had at least two different movies made about her life. She might be the most famous person with autism in the world.

Pictured above: Temple Grandin giving a lecture in 2010.

people with ASD. Because the little icons spell out what emotion is being expressed, someone with ASD doesn't have to struggle to guess. Online, people with autism can find communities of other people who share their enthusiasm about almost any obscure interest. And they can do all these things without having to deal with going out in public.

EDUCATIONAL VIDEO

Scan this code for a talk by Temple Grandin.

Technology has made life easier in other ways for people with developmental disabilities. People with dysgraphia can use a tablet or laptop to type out their work instead of having to struggle with handwriting. People with dyscalculia have instant access to help with math via the calculator app that comes standard on phones, tablets, and computers.

For people with dyslexia or visual disabilities, there has been an explosion of assistive devices and technologies. Text-to-speech functions on smartphones and computers allow someone to hear what's displayed on a screen instead of reading

Emojis can be easier for some people with ASD to understand than human faces are.

it. Scanning pen devices can convert printed materials like books and worksheets to speech. Libraries and subscription services offer a huge variety of audiobooks. Specially designed fonts can help someone with dyslexia read with less effort. They may be downloaded for use on a computer or smartphone, or added as a browser extension to make it easier to surf the web. Apps and word processing programs can allow you to write by converting your spoken word to text. There are even special apps that check writing for common dyslexic phonetic and spelling errors.

Many of these technologies were designed by people with dyslexia and other disabilities to help themselves succeed at school and at work. Because people with developmental disabilities often have problems getting organized and managing their time effectively, many apps are designed to assist with scheduling and getting tasks done.

Technology has made a huge impact on the autism community, creating new ways for people to learn, focus, and organize tasks.

SELF-ADVOCACY

Most diseases, disorders, and health conditions have one or more advocacy groups. These organizations raise funds for research. They lobby federal, state, and local government for laws and policies that will benefit people with the health condition. They make information available, and recommend treatments.

For many years, advocacy groups for developmental disabilities like autism were made up solely of parents of kids with autism, with no contributions from autistic people themselves. But Ari Ne'eman decided to change that. As a high-functioning autistic child, he suffered from many problems common to kids with autism, including trouble in social situations, anxiety, and sensory overload. For a while, he was sent to a special education high school, but he successfully lobbied to return to a more academically rigorous regular high school. That experience inspired him to found the Autism Self Advocacy Network (ASAN), the first advocacy organization staffed and run by people with autism. It produces policy papers, reports, books, videos, and other resource materials for high-functioning people with autism. In 2010 Ne'eman became the first person with autism to serve on the National Council on Disability, a federal agency that advises all levels of government on disability policies. Ne'eman believes that people with autism should be a part of any conversation about autism.

These apps don't just help high-functioning people. Tablet and phone apps for people with intellectual disabilities allow families and caretakers to create visual, step-by-step to-do lists and schedules using icons and photos. These apps can also address learning challenges faced by people with intellectual disabilities.

REVERSING MYTHS ABOUT DYSLEXIA

You may have heard bad jokes about dyslexia. The punchline is usually a word spelled backwards. Those jokes are based on a myth. Dyslexia doesn't make people read, write, or spell backwards. But if dyslexia isn't about writing backwards, then what is it?

Dyslexia is a language-based learning disability with neurobiological causes. That means that it's rooted in the way the brain develops and processes information about language. People with dyslexia do have trouble reading and spelling. They have trouble matching letters to sounds, and may mix them up. They may struggle to name letters of the alphabet, and fail to recognize words even when they've seen them many times before.

The extra time they need to recognize words causes them to read very slowly. Reading so slowly can make it harder to remember what they've read from one page to the next. As very young children, they may have difficulty distinguishing the sounds of words, and they may not understand how to make rhymes. They may also have difficulty with math, handwriting, time management, and organization. But none of this affects how smart they are. People with dyslexia can be very gifted.

People with dyslexia can and do learn to read, but it takes more effort. There are specially designed programs to help kids with dyslexia achieve grade-level reading proficiency. Many people with dyslexia have gone on to do amazing things, including the boxer Muhammad Ali, the actor Orlando Bloom, Nobel Prize winner Carol Greider, and author Dav Pilkey.

In 1966, the champion boxer Muhammad Ali returned to visit the high school where he'd struggled with dyslexia.

Neurodiversity

As more people with developmental disabilities connect to one another, many of them are discovering that they have a lot in common. Rather than define themselves by what they can't do, many of them have decided to celebrate the things they can do. They also celebrate the ways in which they are different from neurotypical people. Instead of thinking of their conditions as disorders, they think of them as differences that exist on a wide continuum of normal human variation. The term **neurodiversity** was coined to express the idea that people should be valued for who they are, regardless of whether they think and behave the way "typical" people do. Neurodiversity activists think scientists shouldn't try to find a cure for developmental disabilities, because there is nothing wrong with thinking and behaving differently. They say that brains develop in different ways, and these ways aren't better or worse than one another—just different.

The idea of neurodiversity is controversial. Some critics argue it erases the suffering of low-functioning people with developmental disabilities, who can't independently manage basic life tasks or communication. Other critics say that even high-functioning people would have a higher quality of life if there was a cure for some impairments. But even if people can't agree on whether to hope for a cure for developmental disabilities, we can all agree that we're better off living in a world in which everyone can live life to the fullest and achieve their goals, regardless of ability.

Text-Dependent Questions

1. What are some jobs that may be good fits for qualities often possessed by people with autism?
2. How has technology made it easier for people with ASD to communicate?
3. What are some technological innovations that can help someone with dyslexia?

Research Project

Some movie theaters offer a "Sensory Friendly Films" program. They provide special showings of popular movies for people with autism and their families. You can read more about them on the Autism Society website, at www.autism-society.org/get-involved/ other-ways-to-get-involved/sensory-friendly-films/. What other "sensory friendly" events can you imagine? Pick one and describe how you would make it more accessible for people with ASD or other developmental disabilities.

FURTHER READING

Abeel, Samantha. *My Thirteenth Winter: A Memoir*. New York: Scholastic, 2005.

Autism Society. "Living with Autism." http://www.autism-society.org/living-with-autism.

Higashida, Naoki. *The Reason I Jump: The Inner Voice of a Thirteen-Year-Old Boy with Autism*. Translated by K. A. Yoshida and David Mitchell. New York: Random House, 2013.

Margulies, Phillip. *Down Syndrome*. New York: Rosen, 2007.

Parks, Peggy J. *Autism*. San Diego, CA: ReferencePoint Press, 2009.

Tabone, Francis. *Autism Spectrum Disorder: The Ultimate Teen Guide*. Lanham, MD: Rowman & Littlefield, 2016.

Verdick, Elizabeth, and Elizabeth Reeve. *The Survival Guide for Kids With Autism Spectrum Disorders (And Their Parents)*. Minneapolis, MN: Free Spirit Publishing, 2015.

Educational Videos

Chapter One: Real Look Autism. "Communication Device." https://www.youtube.com/watch?v=oIGrxzPMVtw.

Chapter Two: Autistic Self Advocacy Network. "Welcome to the Autistic Community." https://www.youtube.com/watch?v=XnuGPJ7UdpU.

Chapter Three: Elliott de Neve. "Dyslexia: The World the Way I See It." https://www.youtube.com/watch?v=rhygmurIgG0.

Chapter Four: Temple Grandin. "The World Needs All Kinds of Minds." https://www.ted.com/talks/temple_grandin_the_world_needs_all_kinds_of_minds?language=en#t-279220.

SERIES GLOSSARY

accommodation: an arrangement or adjustment to a new situation; for example, schools make accommodations to help students cope with illness.

anemia: an illness caused by a lack of red blood cells.

autoimmune: type of disorder where the body's immune system attacks the body's tissues instead of germs.

benign: not harmful.

biofeedback: a technique used to teach someone how to control some bodily functions.

capillaries: tiny blood vessels that carry blood from larger blood vessels to body tissues.

carcinogens: substances that can cause cancer to develop.

cerebellum: the back part of the brain; it controls movement.

cerebrum: the front part of the brain; it controls many higher-level thinking and functions.

cholesterol: a waxy substance associated with fats that coats the inside of blood vessels, causing cardiovascular disease.

cognitive: related to conscious mental activities, such as learning and thinking.

communicable: transferable from one person to another.

congenital: a condition or disorder that exists from birth.

correlation: a connection between different things that suggests they may have something to do with one another.

dominant: in genetics, a dominant trait is expressed in a child even when the trait is only inherited from one parent.

environmental factors: anything that affects how people live, develop, or grow. Climate, diet, and pollution are examples.

genes: units of hereditary information.

hemorrhage: bleeding from a broken blood vessel.

hormones: substances the body produces to instruct cells and tissues to perform certain actions.

inflammation: redness, swelling, and tenderness in a part of the body in response to infection or injury.

insulin: a hormone produced in the pancreas that controls cells' ability to absorb glucose.

lymphatic system: part of the human immune system; transports white blood cells around the body.

malignant: harmful; relating to tumors, likely to spread.

mutation: a change in the structure of a gene; some mutations are harmless, but others may cause disease.

neurological: relating to the nervous system (including the brain and spinal cord).

neurons: specialized cells found in the central nervous system (the brain and spinal cord).

occupational therapy: a type of therapy that teaches one how to accomplish tasks and activities in daily life.

oncology: the study of cancer.

orthopedic: dealing with deformities in bones or muscles.

prevalence: how common or uncommon a disease is in any given population.

prognosis: the forecast for the course of a disease that predicts whether a person with the disease will get sicker, recover, or stay the same.

progressive disease: a disease that generally gets worse as time goes on.

psychomotor: relating to movement or muscle activity resulting from mental activity.

recessive: in genetics, a recessive trait will only be expressed if a child inherits it from both parents.

remission: an improvement in or disappearance of someone's symptoms of disease; unlike a cure, remission is usually temporary.

resilience: the ability to bounce back from difficult situations.

seizure: an event caused by unusual brain activity resulting in physical or behavior changes.

syndrome: a condition with a set of associated symptoms.

ulcers: a break or sore in skin or tissue where cells disintegrate and die. Infections may occur at the site of an ulcer.

INDEX

Illlustrations are indicated by page numbers in *italic* type.

A

abilities, 12, 18, 47, 56
accommodations, 36, 42, 43
acquired mutations, 26, 28
advocacy, 25, 46, 53
aides, dedicated, 12, 42
Ali, Muhammad, 54, *55*
anti–vaccine scam, 31, 32–33
anxiety, 23, 35, 38
apps, 51, 52, 53
articulate, 24, 30
Asperger, Hans, 18
Asperger's syndrome, 18
assistive devices, 24, 28, 51
attention–deficit hyperactivity disorder
     (ADHD), 23, 38
atypical, 8, 16
audiobooks, 52
auditory processing disorder, 15, 33, 34–35
Autism Self Advocacy Network (ASAN),
     53
autism spectrum disorder (ASD), 9, 24–35
  anti–vaccine scam, 32
  background, 11, 12, 22
  causes of, 26, 28
  defined, 28–31, 32–33
  prevalence of, 27
  quotient, 34
  symptoms, *38*
  and tuberous sclerosis complex, 20–21
  understanding, 18
Autistic Spectrum Quotient, 34
awareness, 25

B

babies, *16*, 22, 31
behavior training and therapy, 21, 36, 39
Bleuler, Eugen, 11
Bloom, Orlando, 54
body language, 31
brain functioning, 21
brain injuries, 17
bullying, 41, 50

C

calculator app, 51
categorization, 30
causes
  autism spectrum disorder, 26, 28
  Down syndrome, 15, 16, 22
  dyslexia, 54
  epilepsy, 20
  intellectual disability, 22
  of tuberous sclerosis complex, 20–21
Centers for Disease Control and Prevention
     (CDC), 15
childhood schizophrenia, 11
chromosomes, 8, 15, 16, 22
communication, 28, 30, 39, 49
compelled, feeling, 8, 21
computers, 28, 30, 49
context, 31, 41
continuum, 8, 18
co–occurring conditions, 23
coping skills, 37
costs, *43*
cures, 10, 55, 56

D

delusions, 11

de novo mutations, 26, 28

details, focusing on, 40

developmental disabilities, 8–23

    autism spectrum, 18, *19*

    background, 9

    categories of, 12

    and other disorders, 19–23

    types of, 14–18

    understanding, 10–14

deviation, 36, 37

diagnosis, 9, 28

Diagnostic and Statistical Manual of Mental Disorders (DSM), 11

diets, 38

differences, 41, 46–56, 53

    background, 47

    neurodiversity, 55–56

    self–advocacy and, 53

    technology and, 49, 51–52

digestive problems, 38

direct observation, 28

disability. *see* developmental disabilities

discoveries, 38, 47

Down syndrome, 9, 15–16, 20, 22, 41

dyscalculia, 15, 41, 51

dysgraphia, *14*, 15, 51

dyslexia, 9, 15, 41, 43, 52, 54

E

early treatment, 39

echolalia, 36, 41–42

education, 12, 42–45

Education for All Handicapped Children Act, 44

emojis, 49, 51

emotional connections, 11

emotions, 30, 31

enhanced ability, 46, 47

enrichment programs, 42

environmental factors, 24, 26, 28

epidemic, 27

epilepsy, 19, 20

evaluations, *29*, 34

exaggeration, 31

extreme autistic aloneness, 11

F

face–blind, 31, 32–33

facial expressions, *30*, 31

feeble-minded, homes for, 17

feelings, 8, 21, 30, 41

fetal alcohol spectrum disorder, 16

figurative language, 24, 31

fragile X syndrome, 16, 20

frustration, 30

fund raising, 53

G

genes, 22

genetic conditions, 20–21

genetic mutations, 24, 26, 28

genius, 18

Grandin, Temple, 50

Greider, Carol, 54

growth rate, 22

H

heart defects, 22

high–functioning people, 30

homes for the feeble-minded, 17

hormones, 24, 28

I

idiocy, 17

impairment, 8, 9, 37

inconclusive science, 36, 38

Individualized Education Program (IEP), 42, 43

Individuals with Disabilities Education Act (IDEA), 42, 44–45

infantile autism, 11

information processing, 18, 34–35

inherited mutations, 28

insanity, 17

institutions, 17

intellectual disabilities, 12, 15, 17, 18, 20, 22

intelligence, 12, 18

interests, 11, 30, 32, 33, 49, 51

irony, 31

J

job performance, *48*

jokes, 54

K

Kanner, Leo, 11, 18

Kanner's syndrome, 18

L

language processing disorder, 15

learning disabilities, 12, 14–15, 21, 41

little professors, 18

lobbying, 53

M

maladie de tics, 21

managing activities, 10, 12

measles, 32

media, 25, 27, 49

medications, *20*, 21, 35, 37–38

memorization, 41–42

mental retardation, 15

metaphors, 31

MMR vaccine, 32

motor skills, 42

mumps, 32

muscle tone, 22, 42

mutations, 24, 26, 28

N

National Council on Disability, 53

Ne'eman, Ari, 53

networking, 49

neurobiology, 54

neurodiversity, 46, 55–56

neurotypical, 24, 31, 32–33, 54

nonverbal communication, 31, 39

nonverbal learning disabilities, 15

nutrition, 37–38

nutritional supplements, 36, 38

O

obsessive–compulsive disorder, 23, 35

occupational therapy, 36, 42

one-on-one therapy, 39

organizing, *33*, 52

P

parents, 26, 28

participation, 37

pathologists, speech–language, 36, 39–40

pervasive developmental disorders, 11

physical characteristics, 22

physical coordination, 42

physical therapy, 42

Pilkey, Dav, 54

prevalence of diseases, 8, 15, 27

psychiatric disorders, 24, 35

Q

quality of life, 38

R

repetitive behaviors, 11, 21, 33, 34–35

research, 38, *43*, 47, 49

routine, 33, 34–35

rubella, 32

S

Sacks, Oliver, 50

sarcasm, 31

scanning pen devices, 52

scheduling, 52, 53

schizophrenia, 11

schools, developmental disabilities at, 42, 43–45

screening, 25

seizures, 19, 20

self–advocacy, 53

self–harming behaviors, 35

self–stimulation, 35

sensory information, 34–35

services, 43, 44, 50

sharing, 32–33

similes, 31

skills, 12

smartphones, 51

social communication, 31, 39

social connections, 11

speaking, 30, 39

special education, 12, 42, 43, 45

spectrum, 8, 18, *19*

speech disorders, 23

speech–language therapies, 36, 39–40, 41–42

speech therapy, 39, 42, 50

spoken language, 28, 30

squeeze machine, 50

stimming, 24, 35

stimulation, 34–35

studying, *13*

supplements, nutritional, 36, 38

support, 12, 14, 22

swearing, 21

symptoms, 20, 21, *38*

T

tantrums, 30, 34

technology, 49, 51–52

text-to-speech functions, 51

therapies, *10*, 12, 36–45

    background, 37

    behavior training, 21, 36, 39

    education accommodations, 42, 43–45

    medication and nutrition, 37–38

    other types of, 42

    speech–language, 39, 40, 41–42

tics, 8, 11, 21

Time, 50

time management, 52

toddlers, 31, 32–33

Tourette, George Gilles de la, *21*

Tourette syndrome, 21

tuberous sclerosis complex (TSC), 20–21

tumors, 20–21

21st chromosome, 22

typical people, 54

V

vaccinations, 32

verbal communication, 28, 39

visual perception/visual motor deficit, 15

W

Wakefield, Andrew, 32

word processing programs, 52

X

X chromosome, 16

ABOUT THE ADVISOR

Heather Pelletier, Ph.D., is a pediatric staff psychologist at Rhode Island Hospital/Hasbro Children's Hospital with a joint appointment as a clinical assistant professor in the departments of Psychiatry and Human Behavior and Pediatrics at the Warren Alpert Medical School of Brown University. She is also the director of behavioral pain medicine in the division of Children's Integrative therapies, Pain management and Supportive care (CHIPS) in the department of Pediatrics at Hasbro Children's Hospital. Dr. Pelletier provides clinical services to children in various medical specialty clinics at Hasbro Children's Hospital, including the pediatric gastroenterology, nutrition, and liver disease clinics.

ABOUT THE AUTHOR

Rebecca Sherman writes about health care policy, public health issues, and parenting. She lives in Massachusetts with her family.

PHOTO CREDITS

Cover: iStock/imagesbybarbara
iStock: 10 FatCamera; 14 DragonImages; 16 DenKuvaiev ; 19 alexeys; 20 IPGGutenbergUKLtd ; 22 asiseeit; 26 littleny; 27 jaminwell; 29 gpointstudio; 30 ozgurdonmaz; 38 Geber86; 40 alexsokolov; 41 GeorgiaCourt; 43 Geber86; 48 PeopleImages; 51 yuoak; 52 mixetto
Library of Congress: 55
Shutterstock: 13 Lisa F. Young; 33 PhotoUG
Wikimedia: 50 Steve Jurvetson

J 618.92 SHER
Sherman, Rebecca,
Autism and other
developmental disorders /

JUN 2 5 2018